Teaching Notes

Contents

Making a Book

Romans

Survival

Working in Films

Odd Eggs

Skeletons

Carnegie Primary
School

Introduction

Fireflies is an exciting non-fiction series within *Oxford Reading Tree*. These books are specially designed to be used alongside the Stage 10 stories. They provide practice of reading skills in a non-fiction context whilst using the same simple, repetitive sentence structures as the *Oxford Reading Tree* stories. They also contain a selection of decodable and tricky words. Each stage builds on the reading skills and vocabulary from previous stages. Each book offers scope for developing children's word recognition and language comprehension skills in a highly motivating way, whilst also providing strong cross-curricular links.

To help children approach each new book in this stage with confidence, you should prepare the children for reading by talking about the book and asking questions. You can use these Teaching Notes and the additional notes in the inside front and back covers of the pupil books to help you. The notes within the pupil books can also be used by parents or teaching assistants.

Using the books

This booklet provides suggestions for using the books for guided, group and independent activities. The reading activities include ideas for developing children's *word recognition* **W** and *language comprehension* **C** skills. Within word recognition, there are ideas for helping children practise their phonic skills and knowledge, as well as helping them tackle words which are not easy to decode phonically. The language comprehension ideas include suggestions for teaching the skills of prediction, questioning, clarifying, summarising and imagining, in order to help children understand the texts. Suggestions are also provided for speaking and listening and writing activities, as well as for introducing linked electronic material and cross-curricular links.

Reading fluency

To support children in developing fluency in their reading, you can give them plenty of opportunities to revisit the books. These include:

- rereading independently
- rereading with a partner
- rereading at home
- hearing the book read to them as they follow the printed text.

Rereading and rehearing helps children develop automatic word recognition and gives them models of fluent, expressive reading.

Comprehension strategies

Title	Comprehension strategy taught through these Teaching Notes				
	Prediction	Questioning	Clarifying	Summarising	Imagining
Making a Book	✓	✓	✓	✓	
Romans	✓	✓	✓		✓
Survival	✓	✓	✓	✓	
Working in Films	✓	✓	✓	✓	✓
Odd Eggs	✓	✓	✓		
Skeletons	✓	✓	✓	✓	✓

Vocabulary and phonic opportunities

This chart shows the main words used in each book. The decodable words listed should be decoded for most children at this Stage. The tricky words are common but do not conform to the phonic rules taught up to this point – children will need support to learn and recognise them. If children struggle with one of these words you can model how to read it.

Making a Book	High frequency decodable words	different, illustrations, information, photographs, special
	High frequency tricky words	designer, encyclopedias, graphic, guidebooks, manuscript, researcher
Romans	High frequency decodable words	beginning, calendar, special, unusual, usually
	High frequency tricky words	charioteer, mediterranean, mosaic, patrician, plebian, social, wealthy
Survival	High frequency decodable words	aeroplanes, amazing, dangerous, difference, mountains, prepared, searching
	High frequency tricky words	accidents, avalanche, parachute, rations, saliva, yacht
Working in Films	High frequency decodable words	dangerous, enormous, industry, separately, working
	High frequency tricky words	audition, character, designer, location, scenes
Odd Eggs	High frequency decodable words	different, fossilized, successful, touch, valuable
	High frequency tricky words	cosmetics, cylinders, extraordinary, measure, tsar
Skeletons	High frequency decodable words	different, important, skeleton, special, supports, together
	High frequency tricky words	attached, balance

Curriculum coverage chart

	Speaking and listening activities	Reading	Writing
Making a Book			
PNS Literacy Framework (Y2)	1.3	Ⓦ 6.1 Ⓒ 7.1, 7.3, 8.3	9.1, 9.5
National Curriculum	Working within level 2		
Scotland (5–14) (P3)	Level A/B		
N. Ireland (P3/Y3)	1, 2, 5, 6, 10	2, 3, 4, 6, 8, 9, 11, 15, 16, 17	1, 2, 3, 4, 6, 8, 11
Wales (Key Stage 1)	Range: 1, 3 Skills: 1, 2, 3, 4	Range: 1, 2, 3 Skills: 1, 2, 4	Range: 1, 2, 3, 4, 5, 7 Skills: 1, 3, 5, 6, 7, 8
	Speaking and listening activities	**Reading**	**Writing**
Romans			
PNS Literacy Framework (Y2)	1.3, 4.1	Ⓦ 6.1, 6.2 Ⓒ 7.3	9.4, 10.1, 11.3
National Curriculum	Working within level 2		
Scotland (5–14) (P3)	Level A/B		
N. Ireland (P3/Y3)	1, 2, 4, 5, 6, 7, 8, 10	1, 2, 3, 4, 8, 9, 10, 11, 15, 16, 17	1, 3, 4, 5, 6, 8, 10, 11
Wales (Key Stage 1)	Range: 1, 3, 5 Skills: 1, 2, 4	Range: 1, 2, 4 Skills: 1, 2, 4	Range: 1, 2, 3, 4, 5, 6, 7 Skills: 1, 2, 5, 6, 7, 8

Key

Ⓒ = Language comprehension   Y = Year

Ⓦ = Word recognition   P = Primary

In the designations such as 1.2, the first number represents the strand and the second number the bullet point.

Curriculum coverage chart

	Speaking and listening activities	Reading	Writing
Survival			
PNS Literacy Framework (Y2)	1.3, 3.2	**W** 6.1 **C** 7.1, 7.3, 7.4	11.2
National Curriculum	Working within level 2		
Scotland (5–14) (P3)	Level A/B		
N. Ireland (P3/Y3)	1, 2, 5, 6, 8, 9, 10, 11, 14	1, 2, 9, 15, 16, 17	1, 6, 7, 10, 11, 12, 13
Wales (Key Stage 1)	Range: 1, 2, 3 Skills: 1, 2, 4	Range: 1, 2, 3, 4 Skills: 1, 2, 4	Range: 1, 2, 3, 4, 7 Skills: 1, 3, 7, 8
	Speaking and listening activities	Reading	Writing
Working in Films			
PNS Literacy Framework (Y2)	1.3, 3.1, 3.3	**W** 6.1 **C** 7.3, 7.4	9.1, 9.3, 9.5
National Curriculum	Working within level 2		
Scotland (5–14) (P3)	Level A/B		
N. Ireland (P3/Y3)	1, 2, 5, 6, 7, 8, 10, 11	2, 3, 8, 15, 16, 17	1, 3, 5, 6, 8, 10
Wales (Key Stage 1)	Range: 1, 3 Skills: 1, 2, 3, 4	Range: 1, 2, 4 Skills: 1, 2, 4	Range: 1, 3, 4, 5, 6, 7 Skills: 1, 3, 5, 6, 7, 8

Curriculum coverage chart

	Speaking and listening activities	Reading	Writing
Odd Eggs			
PNS Literacy Framework (Y2)	1.3, 3.1, 3.2	**W** 6.1 **C** 7.1, 7.3, 8.1, 8.3	9.1, 9.5, 11.1, 11.2
National Curriculum	Working towards level 2		
Scotland (5–14) (P3)	Level A/B		
N. Ireland (P3/Y3)	1, 2, 5, 6, 8, 10	2, 8, 9, 11, 15, 16, 17	1, 3, 5, 6, 8, 11
Wales (Key Stage 1)	Range: 1, 3 Skills: 1, 2, 4	Range: 1, 2, 3, 4 Skills: 1, 2, 3, 4	Range: 1, 3, 4, 7 Skills: 1, 2, 5, 7, 8
	Speaking and listening activities	**Reading**	**Writing**
Skeletons			
PNS Literacy Framework (Y2)	3.1	**W** 6.1 **C** 7.1, 7.3, 7.4	9.3, 9.5
National Curriculum	Working towards level 2		
Scotland (5–14) (P3)	Level A/B		
N. Ireland (P3/Y3)	1, 2, 5, 6, 9, 10, 14	2, 8, 9, 15, 16, 17	2, 3, 6, 8, 10, 12
Wales (Key Stage 1)	Range: 1, 2, 3 Skills: 1, 2, 3, 4	Range: 1, 2 Skills: 1, 2, 4	Range: 1, 2, 4, 5, 7 Skills: 1, 3, 5, 6, 7, 8

Making a Book

> C = Language comprehension   *R, AF* = QCA reading assessment focus
>
> W = Word recognition   *W, AF* = QCA writing assessment focus

Group or guided reading

Introducing the book

C *(Prediction, Questioning)* Look together at the cover. Ask the children to read the title and the name of the author, and to predict the content of the book. Is it fiction or non-fiction?

C *(Clarifying)* Ask the children to flick through the book to confirm their predictions. Ask them to give a reason for their answer.

W Ask the children to find the Contents page and read the headings together.

C *(Questioning, Clarifying)* Look through the book, focusing on the headings. Ask the children to say what this book is about. Is it about horses or producing a book? Explain that the headings are followed by information that explains the process of making a book.

Strategy check

Remind the children to use their knowledge of phonics in decoding longer words.

Independent reading

C *(Questioning)* Ask the children to explain how the illustrations in this book give readers a clue as to whether it is fiction or non-fiction.

W Remind the children to use their decoding skills when they encounter a difficult word and to check their reading of it makes sense in the context. Ask them how the visual information supports and enhances their understanding of the text.

C *(Questioning, Clarifying)* Ask the children to talk about the flow chart on pages 6 and 7. Is this an effective way to explain what a publishing team consists of?

Check that children:

- *(R, AF1)* use a variety of strategies to work out new words
- *(R, AF4)* use an awareness of grammar to decipher new or unfamiliar words
- *(R, AF3)* understand the distinction between fact and fiction; use the terms 'fact', 'fiction' and 'non-fiction' appropriately.

Returning to the text

Ⓒ *(Clarifying)* Discuss whether readers would benefit more from reading this book in the order of the chapter headings, or by dipping in for specific information.

Ⓒ *(Questioning, Summarising)* Ask the children if this book has given them a clear understanding of the publishing process. Can they name some of the basic stages?

Ⓦ Ensure they understand new vocabulary by asking them to explain a chapter heading to you, e.g. What are 'first layouts'?

- Ask the children to scan the text to find and identify vocabulary used to show a process, e.g. 'first', 'then', 'after', 'when', 'lastly', 'finally'.

Group and independent reading activities

Objective Explain organisational features of texts, including alphabetical order (7.3).

Ⓒ *(Questioning, Clarifying)* Ask the children to look at the Contents page and then the Index, and to discuss how they differ.

- Discuss how an alphabetically ordered list can allow a reader to focus on specific information quickly and easily.
- Ask the children to find the page reference number for 'font', without reading down the whole list, and to find the correct page (page 20).
- Ask children to choose a word from the Index, and their partners to find and read the sentence or sentences containing the word, and to make notes on what they have found out.

Assessment *(R, AF2)* Do the children find information from the Index quickly and easily?

Objective Explain their reactions to texts, commenting on important aspects (8.3).

- Look at some other non-fiction books and talk about how they were published.
- Ask the children which they prefer in terms of their layout and why.

Assessment *(R, AF2)* Do the children refer to details of the books' layouts when discussing their preferences?

Objective Draw together ideas and information from across a whole text (7.1). Draw on knowledge and experience of texts in deciding and planning what and how to write (9.1).

- **C** *(Clarifying)* Ask the children to find examples in the book of illustrations that have captions and labels.
- Ask them to explain how captions and labels differ.
- Discuss which captions work well and why.
- In pairs children should discuss the information on page 8 and write alternative captions. Discuss which captions provide useful information.

Assessment *(R, AF4)* Do the children understand the purpose of captions?

Objective Spell with increasing accuracy and confidence, drawing on ... spelling patterns (6.1).

- **W** Write several words with the ending 'le' on the board. Ask the children to add other words from their own experience to the list.
- Ask the children to find other 'le' words in the book, e.g. 'sample' (page 8), 'saddle' (page 11), 'example' (page 15).
- Ask the children to add these words to their personal word banks.

Assessment *(R, AF1)* Are the children able to identify and read the words accurately?

Speaking and listening activities

Objective Explain ideas and processes using imaginative and adventurous vocabulary and non-verbal gestures to support communication (1.3).

- Ask the children to bring their favourite book to the group.
- Ask them to explain what sort of book it is (fiction or non-fiction) and to describe the features that show what type of book it is.

Cross-curricular links: National Curriculum Key Stage 1

ICT

Pupils should be taught:

- To present their completed work effectively

Writing activities

Objective Draw on knowledge and experience of texts in deciding and planning how and what to write (9.1).
Select from different presentational features to suit particular writing purposes on paper and on screen (9.5).

- Ask the children to discuss how an alphabetically ordered text on the same subject (making books) would differ from this book.
- Ask the children to work with a partner and draw up a list of terms that they would include in a dictionary of book publishing.
- Provide a selection of dictionaries for the children to use as models.
- The children can write their own short *Dictionary of Making a Book.*
- Use a computer to bring their work to a finished standard.

Assessment *(W, AF3)* Do the children sequence the information correctly and structure the pages effectively?

Romans

> **C** = Language comprehension   *R, AF* = QCA reading assessment focus
>
> **W** = Word recognition   *W, AF* = QCA writing assessment focus

Group or guided reading

Introducing the book

C *(Questioning, Prediction)* Look together at the cover. Ask the children to read the title and author's name and to predict the book's content.

C *(Clarifying)* Ask the children to read the back cover blurb to support their predictions.

C *(Clarifying)* Ask the children to locate the Contents page, Index and Glossary.

W Look through the book and point out any vocabulary that may be challenging, e.g. 'Mediterranean', 'patrician' and 'plebian'.

W Ask the children to read the Contents page. Ask them to find common word endings in the Contents ('–ing' and '–es' endings).

Strategy check

Remind the children to use their knowledge of spelling patterns and context to work out unfamiliar words.

Independent reading

C *(Questioning)* Ask the children to find and read the pages that describe 'Living in the City' and 'Living in the Country'. Ask them if the order in which these pages are read is important.

W Remind the children to use the Glossary to check unknown terms.

C *(Questioning)* Ask them how the visual information supports and enhances their understanding of the text.

Assessment Check that children:

- *(R, AF1)* use a variety of strategies to work out new words
- *(R, AF1)* read the decodable words listed on page 4 of these notes fluently

- (R, AF3) understand that chronological order is not always important in understanding the information in non-fiction writing
- (R, AF2) use the Contents page to find specific pages.

Returning to the text

C (Questioning) Ask the children questions, such as: *What did Roman boys and girls wear? Can you name two toys Roman children played with?* Ensure they use the Contents or Index to find their answers.

C (Clarifying) Ask children to name the non-fiction features in the book.

W Ask: *Which words were hard to read? How did you work them out?*

C (Clarifying) Can the children explain why there are only a few photographs used in this non-fiction text?

C (Imagining) Ask: *Would life have been difficult or fun in Roman times?* Ask them to give their reasons by referring to the text.

Group and independent reading activities

Objective Explain organisational features of texts (7.3).

C (Questioning, Clarifying) Ask the children to read the information in the chart on page 5.

- Discuss how a chart can be useful in giving brief information in an accessible way, but that narrative text can give more detail.
- Ask the children to use the Contents page or the Index to find other information about schools and homes.
- Ask them to make notes describing the extra information that is in the text but not in the chart.

Assessment (R, AF4) Do the children understand why the book uses both a chart and narrative text?

Objective Spell with increasing accuracy and confidence (6.1). Use question marks (11.3).

W Ask the children to work with a partner. Ask them to write five questions about the Romans on a piece of paper, and swap them with their partner.

- Ask them to write down the page reference where each answer is to be found.

Assessment *(W, AF8)* Do the children use correct spelling?

Assessment *(W, AF2)* Do the children remember to use question marks?

Objective Spell with increasing accuracy and confidence, drawing on ... knowledge of word structure (6.1).

W Can children spot words with common endings (e.g. '–ing', '–ed' and '–s')? Encourage them to spell them out for you to write on the board.

Assessment *(W, AF8)* Do the children use correct spellings?

Objective Read and spell less common alternative graphemes (6.2).

W Use the Glossary and Index as a list of new spellings to practise. Ask the children to add other words from the text that they are unsure of.

- Ask the children to add these words to their personal word banks.

Assessment *(R, AF1)* Do the children use their phonic knowledge to tackle words with less familiar graphemes?

E-links

Fireflies Plus

If you are an Espresso user, you can access videos, quizzes and activities linked to this title to enrich your children's reading. Children can also write, post and compare reviews of the book. Full supporting Teaching Notes for this content are available on the site in PDF format. Within the Espresso site, follow the route **<Channel guide → English 1 → Oxford Reading Tree Fireflies Plus logo>**. *Espresso Primary* is an extensive library of cross-curricular, video-rich broadband teaching resources and learning activities that motivates children and supports teachers.

Speaking and listening activities

Objective Explain ideas and processes using imaginative and adventurous vocabulary (1.3).

Adopt appropriate roles in small or large groups (4.1).

- Ask the children to read and discuss the information on pages 4 and 5.
- Ask four children to take the roles of a patrician, an equite, a plebian and a slave, and to sit in the 'hot-seat'. Ask the remaining children to ask them questions about their roles in society and how they feel, think and act.

Cross-curricular links: National Curriculum Key Stage 1

History

Pupils should be taught to:
- Identify differences between ways of life at different times.

Writing activities

Objective Make adventurous word and language choices appropriate to the style and purpose of the text (9.4).
Use planning to establish clear sections for writing (10.1).

- Ask the children to make notes about each separate social group in Roman times.
- They should make notes of key words, phrases or information to use when describing the group.
- The children write a description of one of the social groups, using their own words.
- Collect the finished pages to make a group or class book on the topic.

Assessment *(W, AF3)* Do the children structure their book and use presentational features effectively?

Survival

C = Language comprehension	*R, AF* = QCA reading assessment focus	
W = Word recognition	*W, AF* = QCA writing assessment focus	

Group or guided reading

Introducing the book

C *(Questioning, Prediction)* Look together at the cover. Ask the children to read the title and the name of the author, and to predict the content of the book. Is it fiction or non-fiction? Ask them to give a reason for their opinions.

W Ask the children to locate the Contents page and read the headings.

W Discuss the meaning of the words 'survival' and 'survivor'. Ask the children to scan the pages to find these words in the text.

Strategy check

Remind the children to use their knowledge of phonics and context to work out new words.

Independent reading

C *(Questioning)* Ask the children to read the Introduction, and then to read two different survival stories.

C *(Clarifying)* Ask them if the order these pages are read in is important in understanding the information.

W Ask the children to find another word with a similar spelling pattern and meaning to that of 'survival' (i.e. 'survive').

C *(Questioning)* Ask them to say how important they feel the visual information is to the text.

Assessment Check that children:

- *(R, AF1)* use a variety of strategies to work out new words
- *(R, AF1)* recognise the spelling pattern in 'survive', 'survival' and 'survivor'

- (R, AF4) understand that chronological order is not always important in understanding the information.

Returning to the text

C (Summarising) To ensure children have understood the information in the text, ask them to summarise the content of the book.

W Ask the children to find the word 'amazing' on page 3. Can the children find any different examples that use the root word 'amaze'? ('amazingly' on pages 5 and 12)

W Together, write a list of the sort of people who help us survive accidents, e.g. policemen, firemen, lifeboat men. Check the children's spelling.

W Discuss the use of verbs in the survival stories. Ask the children to explain the difference in verb tenses in the Introduction and the remainder of the text.

Group and independent reading activities

Objective Explain organisational features of texts, including alphabetical order (7.3).

Use syntax and context to build their store of vocabulary (7.4).

C (Questioning) Ask the children to look at the Contents page and then the Index, and to discuss how they differ.

C (Clarifying) Discuss how an alphabetically ordered list can allow a reader to focus on specific information quickly and easily.

W Ask the children to find the page reference number for 'mountain' on the Contents page, without reading down the whole list, and to find the correct page.

W Ask them to choose a word from the Index and their partner to find and read the sentence or sentences containing the information.

- Take turns to find information relating to other words in the Index.

Assessment (R, AF1) Can the children find the Index words quickly and read them fluently?

Objective Spell with increasing accuracy and confidence (6.1).

Ⓦ Write sentences from the text on the board or on paper with the verbs omitted, e.g.

Joan's heart _____ .

The car _____ a tree very hard.

They _____ some sugary drinks and they _____ little sips.

● Ask the children to write the missing verbs in the spaces and to check their accuracy against the text.

Assessment *(R, AF1)* Do the children spell the words correctly?

Objective Use syntax and context to build their store of vocabulary (7.4).

Ⓦ Using the verbs the children identified to fill the gaps in the sentences, ask them to write the root verb.

● Ask the children to change the verbs into the continuous present tense.

● Ask the children to add these words to their personal word banks.

Assessment *(W, AF8)* Do the children use correct spellings?

Speaking and listening activities

Objective Explain ideas and processes using imaginative and adventurous vocabulary (1.3).
Work effectively in groups by ensuring that each group member takes a turn challenging, supporting and moving on (3.2).

● Ask the children to suggest what the most important factors were in the survival of the people. Ensure everyone in the group contributes and responds to each individual's ideas.

Cross-curricular links: National Curriculum Key Stage 1

PSHE & citizenship

Pupils should be taught:

- Rules for, and ways of, keeping safe, and about people who can help them to stay safe.

Writing activities

Objective Draw together ideas and information from across a whole text, using simple signposts in the text (7.1).
Compose sentences using tense consistently (present and past) (11.2).

- Ask the children to make notes of the key factors that helped each person survive their accident.

- Ask them to make notes of key words and phrases.

- Draw up a chart and ask the children to transfer their notes onto it, e.g.

	injuries	water	food	rescuers
skydiving				
car crash 1				

- Ask them to write a sentence about the two factors they think were the most important in the survival stories.

Assessment *(W, AF6)* Are the children's sentences written with consistent use of tense?

Working in Films

> **C** = Language comprehension   *R, AF* = QCA reading assessment focus
>
> **W** = Word recognition   *W, AF* = QCA writing assessment focus

Group or guided reading

Introducing the book

C *(Predicting)* Look together at the cover. Ask the children to read the title and the name of the author, and to predict the content of the book. Is it fiction or non-fiction?

C *(Clarifying)* Ask the children to read the back cover blurb to support their predictions.

C *(Clarifying)* Ask the children to locate the Contents page, Glossary and Index.

C *(Clarifying)* Look through the book, focusing on the headings. Explain that each heading is the name given to different jobs in film-making. The heading is followed by details of what the job involves.

W Ask the children to read the Contents page. Ask them to identify common word endings, e.g. '–or' and '–er'.

Strategy check

Remind the children to use their knowledge of phonics and context to work out unfamiliar words.

Independent reading

W Ask the children to find and read the pages that describe the role of a Costume Designer (pages 18–19), then to read about the Casting Director (pages 10–11). Ensure they use a variety of strategies to read fluently.

C *(Questioning)* Ask them if the order these pages are read in is important in understanding the information.

C *(Clarifying)* Remind the children to refer to the Glossary to check the meaning of terms in bold.

(C) *(Questioning)* Ask them how the visual information supports and enhances their understanding of the text.

Assessment Check that children:

- *(R, AF1)* use a variety of strategies to work out new words
- *(R, AF1)* read decodable words fluently
- *(R, AF4)* understand that chronological order is not always important in understanding the information.

Returning to the text

(C) *(Questioning, Imagining)* Ask the children which roles they would prefer and to find the relevant pages that describe the role. Ask them what they would like about the job.

(W) Ask them how the Glossary supports their understanding.

(C) *(Questioning)* Ensure they have understood the information by asking them to explain a section in their own words, e.g. ask: *Why are stunt people used?*

(C) *(Summarising)* Challenge the children to summarise the book in two or three sentences.

Group and independent reading activities

Objective Explain organisational features of texts, including alphabetical order (7.3).

Use syntax and context to build their store of vocabulary (7.4).

(C) *(Clarifying)* Ask the children to look at the Contents page and then the Index, and to discuss how they differ. Discuss how an alphabetically ordered list can allow a reader to focus on specific information quickly and easily.

- Ask the children to find the page reference number for 'location' in the Index, without reading down the whole list, and to find the correct page.

(W) Ask them to choose a word from the Index, and with a partner find and read the sentence, or sentences, containing the word.

Assessment *(R, AF1)* Do the children find the word and read the sentences fluently?

Objective Ensure that everyone contributes, ... consider alternatives and reach agreement (3.1).

Explain organisational features of texts (7.3).

Ⓦ Ask the children to scan the text and find the words that are included in the Glossary. Ask them to explain how they are able to identify the words.

Ⓒ *(Clarifying)* Ask them to work in groups to decide on another technique that could be used to highlight specific vocabulary, e.g. italic print, capital letters, underlining, shading. Ask them to note the reasons for their choice (e.g. colour is too distracting).

● Draw up a list of techniques for use in their own writing.

Assessment *(R, AF4)* Do the children suggest an appropriate technique and give carefully considered reasons for their choice?

Objective Spell with increasing accuracy and confidence (6.1).

Use syntax and context to build their store of vocabulary (7.4).

Ⓦ Use the Index as a list of new spellings to practise. Ask the children to add other words from the text that they are unsure of. Ask the children to add these words to their personal word banks.

Assessment *(R, AF1)* Do the children use their knowledge of spelling conventions?

Speaking and listening activities

Objective Explain ideas and processes using imaginative and adventurous vocabulary (1.3).

Listen to each other's views and preferences (3.3).

Ⓒ *(Imagining)* Discuss the information on page 12. Ask the group to imagine they are actors on a film set and to say what 'strange things' they would like to have during filming and why. Encourage discussion as to why actors ask for such things (e.g. actors know they are in demand, they are rich and famous, etc.) and whether their requests are reasonable.

Cross-curricular links: National Curriculum Key Stage 1

ICT

Pupils should be taught:

- To use text, tables, images and sound to develop their ideas.

Writing activities

Objective Draw on knowledge and experience of texts in deciding and planning what and how to write (9.1).

Maintain consistency in non-narrative including purpose and tense (9.3).

Select from different presentational features to suit particular writing purposes on paper and on screen (9.5).

- Ask the children to reread the pages about different roles in film-making.

- Ask them to make notes of key words, phrases or information to use when describing the role.

- Ask them to select key words for a glossary of terms to help a younger audience access the information.

- On a computer, children write a description of one of the roles in film-making, using their own words and adding a clip-art illustration.

- Collect the finished pages to make a group or class book on the topic.

Assessment *(W, AF2)* Do the children select suitable terms for the glossary? Do they use non-fiction features, such as captions, effectively?

Odd Eggs

C = Language comprehension	*R, AF* = QCA reading assessment focus
W = Word recognition	*W, AF* = QCA writing assessment focus

Group or guided reading

Introducing the book

C *(Prediction)* Look together at the cover. Ask the children to read the title and the name of the author, and to predict the content of the book. Is it fiction or non-fiction? Ask the children to read the back cover blurb to support their predictions.

C *(Questioning, Clarifying)* Ask the children to locate the Contents page, Glossary and Index. Ask the children to read the Contents page.

C *(Prediction)* Look through the book and prompt the children to predict the content of the text by thinking about the illustrations.

W Help the children to pronounce certain words that may cause problems, e.g. 'sturgeon', 'caviar', 'Fabergé', 'Tsar', 'crêpe'.

Strategy check

Remind the children to use their knowledge of sounds and spelling patterns to work out unfamiliar words.

Independent reading

C *(Questioning)* Ask the children to use the Contents page to find the pages about decorating eggs. Can they explain how this differs from the rest of the book?

C *(Questioning, Clarifying)* Ask them if the order these pages are read in is important in understanding the information and to give reasons for their answer.

C *(Questioning, Clarifying)* Ask them how the language and layout changes on pages 14 to 19 are different from the rest of the book.

W Remind the children to refer to the Glossary to check the meaning of unknown terms.

Check that children:

- *(R, AF1)* use a variety of strategies to work out new words
- *(R, AF1)* read high and medium frequency words automatically
- *(R, AF1)* use their knowledge of suffixes to work out longer words
- *(R, AF4)* use the Contents page to find specific pages.

Returning to the text

C *(Questioning)* Ask the children to name the non-fiction features that are included in the book.

W Ask them to identify common suffixes. Talk about how they modify meaning, e.g. ('–est' in 'smallest'/'biggest').

Group and independent reading activities

Objective Draw together ideas and information from across a whole text (7.1). Explain organisational features of texts (7.3).

C *(Questioning, Clarifying)* Ask the children in groups to each write three questions about the information in the text.

- Ask the children to exchange their questions and find a sentence containing the answer using a different method for each question, i.e. from the Contents page, the Index, and by scanning the text.
- Encourage them to say which method they found the most effective.

Assessment *(R, AF4)* Do the children understand the different purposes of the Contents, Glossary and Index and how each is organised?

Objective Read whole books on their own, choosing and justifying selections (8.1). Explain their reactions to texts, commenting on important aspects (8.3).

C *(Questioning, Clarifying)* Ask the children to say which pages they found the most interesting and why. Ask them to list features (e.g. interesting heading, clear text, interesting facts, interesting photos) that caught and held their attention, and why.

Assessment *(R, AF5, AF6)* Do the children refer to examples of text and layout features when expressing their preferences?

Objective Write simple and compound sentences (11.1).

Compose sentences using tense consistently (11.2).

C *(Clarifying)* Ask the children to look at the illustrations in the text and identify whether they have labels or captions.

● Ask them to choose an illustration without a caption and then to look through the text to find a suitable phrase or sentence about it. They should use this text to write a caption for the illustration.

W Discuss which are the most effective captions and why. Can they suggest alternative words or phrases to improve them?

● Can the children explain the difference between captions and labels?

Assessment *(W, AF2)* Are the children's captions clear?

Assessment *(W, AF6)* Are their sentences technically accurate?

Speaking and listening activities

Objective Explain ideas and processes using imaginative and adventurous vocabulary (1.3).

Ensure that everyone contributes (3.1).

Work effectively in groups by ensuring that each group member takes a turn (3.2).

● Ask the children to read the Egg Facts, and then say which one they found most interesting and why.

● Ask them about the ways eggs can be cooked and eaten, and which they prefer.

● Together, work out what instructions are needed to tell someone how to boil/fry/scramble an egg. Talk about how the instructions could be improved.

Cross-curricular links: National Curriculum Key Stage 1

ICT

Pupils should be taught

- To present their completed work effectively.

Writing activities

Objective   Spell with increasing accuracy and confidence (6.1).

Draw on knowledge and experience of texts in deciding and planning what and how to write (9.1).

Select from different presentational features to suit particular writing purposes on paper and on screen (9.5).

- Discuss the language features of instruction texts. Ask the children to identify if any other parts of the book could be written in the style of instructions ('Games with Eggs').

- Ask the children to rewrite pages 20 and 22 as sets of numbered instructions.

- Use computers to combine text and illustrations to bring their work to a finished standard.

Assessment   *(W, AF3)* Do the children use the imperative verb correctly and sequence their instructions logically? Do they spell most words correctly?

Skeletons

> **C** = Language comprehension   *R, AF* = QCA reading assessment focus
>
> **W** = Word recognition   *W, AF* = QCA writing assessment focus

Group or guided reading

Introducing the book

C *(Questioning, Prediction)* Look together at the front cover illustration and read the title and the name of the author. Ask the children to predict the content. Ask them to give a reason for their answer.

C *(Clarifying)* Ask the children to read the back cover blurb to confirm their predictions.

W Look together at the Index and identify any words the children have difficulty with. Ask for suggestions on how to work them out.

C *(Clarifying)* Look through the book, identifying words in bold print. Explain that the meaning of these words can be found in the Glossary.

C *(Clarifying)* Ask the children to locate the Contents page, Glossary and Index.

Strategy check

Remind the children to use their knowledge of phonics and spelling patterns to work out new words.

Independent reading

W After reading page 5, ask the children to identify any common suffixes (e.g. '–est' and '–ing'). Discuss how their addition changes the meaning of the root words.

C *(Clarifying)* Ask the children to read up to page 11, then to use the Index to find six new facts about different aspects of a skeleton.

W Remind the children to refer to the Glossary to check the meaning of unknown terms.

W Ask them how the visual information supports and enhances their understanding of the text.

(C) *(Questioning)* Look at the Index on page 24. Ask: *In what way is it different from the Contents list?*

Assessment   Check that children:

- *(R, AF1)* use a variety of strategies to work out new words
- *(R, AF1)* read on sight high and medium frequency words
- *(R, AF4)* use the Index to find information accurately.

Returning to the text

(C) *(Summarising)* Ask the children to share the information they found using the Index with the group.

(C) *(Clarifying, Imagining)* To ensure their comprehension of the text, ask them to find images of X-rays in the book and explain their purpose.

(C) *(Questioning)* Ask them to explain how broken bones mend.

(W) On page 18, ask the children to find the word 'strong' in the main text and in the 'Bone Fact'. Ask how the '–er' suffix in 'stronger' changes its meaning. Is there another suffix that could be added to 'strong'? ('–est')

(C) *(Summarising)* Ask the children to summarise the contents of the book.

Group and independent reading activities

Objective   Draw together ideas and information from across a whole text (7.1). Explain organisational features of texts, including alphabetical order (7.3).

(C) *(Questioning, Clarifying)* Ask the children to look at the Contents page and then the Index. Ask: *How do they differ?* Discuss how an alphabetically ordered list allows a reader to find information quickly and easily.

(W) Ask the children to find the page reference number for a photograph, without reading down the whole list, and to locate the correct page.

(C) *(Questioning)* Ask them to tell you, in their own words, what the main point of the paragraph is.

Assessment   *(R, AF1)* Do the children find words in the Index and text quickly?

Objective Explain organisational features of texts (7.3).

Spell with increasing accuracy and confidence (6.1).

You will need small reusable stickers for each child.

C *(Clarifying)* Ask the children to look at all the images and identify which ones have captions, and which have captions and labels.

W Ask them to use one of the skeleton pictures (not the one on page 4) to test their knowledge of bone names. Ask them to use the stickers to label the picture. Remind them to check their spellings.

Assessment *(W, AF8)* Do the children use correct spellings for their labels?

Objective Spell with increasing accuracy and confidence, drawing on … spelling patterns (6.1).

Use syntax and context to build their store of vocabulary (7.4).

W Discuss the spelling pattern of the word 'brittle' on page 7. Ask them to scan the text for other words that share this spelling pattern ('little' page 5, 'ankle' page 8, 'muscles' page 12).

● Ask the children to add other words with the same spelling pattern from their own experience, or using a dictionary or word-bank.

Assessment *(W, AF8)* Do the children use correct spellings in their list?

E-links

E-Fireflies

This book is available electronically, on *e-Fireflies* Stages 6–10 CD-ROM. You can use 'Explore a Book' with the children, to help them access screens/pages in different orders and annotate the text using the e-tools. You then have a choice of activities to give the children, which will include a sequencing, matching or writing activity. Use the Teacher Settings screen to select how you want any part of the CD-ROM to be used, and the Progress Report Chart to track the progress of individual children.

Fireflies Plus

If you are an Espresso user, you can access videos, quizzes and activities linked to this title to enrich your children's reading. Children can also write, post and compare reviews of the book. Full supporting

Teaching Notes for this content are available on the site in PDF format. Within the Espresso site, follow the route **<Channel guide → English 1 → Oxford Reading Tree Fireflies Plus logo>**. *Espresso Primary* is an extensive library of cross-curricular, video-rich broadband teaching resources and learning activities that motivates children and supports teachers.

Speaking and listening activities

Objective Ensure that everyone contributes, allocate tasks (3.1).

- Ask the children to work with a partner. Tell each pair of children to work out and present a short oral presentation of the information in the book, with one child speaking and the other acting as a model to illustrate their chosen information.

Cross-curricular links: National Curriculum Key Stage 1

PSHE & citizenship
Pupils should be taught:
- The names of the main parts of the body.

Writing activities

Objective Draw on knowledge and experience of texts in deciding and planning what and how to write (9.1).
Select from different presentational features to suit particular writing purposes on paper and on screen (9.5).

- Discuss how the Index is written as an alphabetical list. Ask: *How could this be used as a basis for a simple book*?

- Discuss the content and structure of alphabetically organised texts they are familiar with, e.g. dictionary, thesaurus, encyclopedia.

- Ask the children to use the information in the text to write an alphabetically ordered text, e.g. an encyclopedia of bones.

Assessment *(W, AF3)* Do the children structure the information effectively?

Oxford Reading Tree resources at this level

Poetry
Glow-worms stages 10–11

Wider reading
Jackdaws Anthologies packs 1, 2 and 3
cross-curricular Jackdaws stages 10–11
Stage 10 Snapdragons

Electronic
eFireflies
ORT Online www.OxfordReadingTree.com

Teachers' Resources
Snapdragons Teaching Notes, Guided
Reading Cards and Parent Notes

OXFORD
UNIVERSITY PRESS

Great Clarendon Street, Oxford OX2 6DP

Oxford University Press is a department of the University of
Oxford. It furthers the University's objective of excellence in
research, scholarship, and education by publishing worldwide in

Oxford   New York
Auckland   Cape Town   Dar es Salaam   Hong Kong   Karachi
Kuala Lumpur   Madrid   Melbourne   Mexico City   Nairobi
New Delhi   Shanghai   Taipei   Toronto

With offices in

Argentina   Austria   Brazil   Chile   Czech Republic   France
Greece   Guatemala   Hungary   Italy   Japan   Poland
Portugal   Singapore   South Korea   Switzerland
Thailand   Turkey   Ukraine   Vietnam

Oxford is a registered trade mark of Oxford University Press
in the UK and in certain other countries

Text © Oxford University Press 2008

Written by Liz Miles

The moral rights of the author have been asserted

Database right Oxford University Press (maker)

First published 2008

British Library Cataloguing in Publication Data

Data available

ISBN 978-0-19-847341-1

10 9 8 7 6 5 4 3

Page make-up by Thomson Digital

Printed in China

Paper used in the production of this book is a natural, recyclable
product made from wood grown in sustainable forests. The
manufacturing process conforms to the environmental
regulations of the country of origin.